Dive into the fascinating  where man defies the m water

From the first bursts of genius in local pools to the epic sprints of the Olympic Games, swimming has spawned legends whose stories transcend the sport itself.

"50 Swimming Legends and Their Stories" invites you to navigate through these tales, discovering the sacrifices, triumphs and moments of ecstasy that have shaped
these exceptional swimmers.

Prepare to be swept away by the current of these inspiring stories and feel the passion that drives each champion.

SUMMARY

#1- MICHAEL PHELPS
#2- IAN THORPE
#3- KATIE LEDECKY
#4- MARK SPITZ
#5- JENNY THOMPSON
#6- KRISTIN OTTO
#7- RYAN LOCHTE
#8- ALEXANDER POPOV
#9- DAWN FRASER
#10- INGE DE BRUIJN
#11- PIETER VAN DEN HOOGENBAND
#12- MISSY FRANKLIN
#13- NATALIE COUGHLIN
#14- MATT BIONDI
#15- LIBBY TRICKETT
#16- GRANT HACKETT
#17- KRISZTINA EGERSZEGI
#18- DEBBIE MEYER
#19- MURRAY ROSE
#20- KIEREN PERKINS
#21- PETRIA THOMAS
#22- CÉSAR CIELO
#23- TRACY CAULKINS
#24- MARY T. MEAGHER
#25- PENNY OLEKSIAK

SUMMARY

#26- SHANE GOULD
#27- FRANZISKA VAN ALMSICK
#28- IAN CROCKER
#29- STEPHANIE RICE
#30- AMANDA BEARD
#31- REBECCA ADLINGTON
#32- AARON PEIRSOL
#33- RANOMI KROMOWIDJOJO
#34- LAURE MANAUDOU
#35- MICHAEL GROSS
#36- YANA KLOCHKOVA
#37- LASZLO CSEH
#38- DARA TORRES
#39- FLORENT MANAUDOU
#40- ADAM PEATY
#41- LEISEL JONES
#42- SARAH SJÖSTRÖM
#43- KOSUKE KITAJIMA
#44- DUNCAN ARMSTRONG
#45- CHAD LE CLOS
#46- SUN YANG
#47- RUTA MEILUTYTE
#48- CAMILLE MUFFAT
#49- OTYLIA JĘDRZEJCZAK
#50- JANET EVANS

#1

MICHAEL PHELPS
"THE FLYING FISH"

BORN JUNE 30, 1985 IN BALTIMORE, MARYLAND, UNITED STATES.

Michael Phelps is the most decorated swimmer in Olympic history. With an impressive total of 28 medals, including 23 gold, he has set records that seem unattainable to most. His signature victories include eight gold medals at the 2008 Beijing Olympics, surpassing the previous record of seven held by Mark Spitz.

THE GOLDEN SHINE OF THE NATATORIUM

Phelps is famous not only for his record number of Olympic medals, but also for his unparalleled swimming technique and dedication to training. His ability to generate phenomenal power, combined with an incredible arm span, has often caused him to be compared to a fish in action.

Phelps' career has been filled with memorable moments. His epic face-to-face with Serbian Milorad Čavić in the 100m butterfly in Beijing, where he won by a hundredth of a second, is legendary. Out of the pool, after the 2012 London Games, he announced his retirement, only to return for the 2016 Rio Games, where he added five gold medals and one silver to his tally. Outside of his aquatic exploits, Phelps has been open about his struggles with depression, becoming a mental health advocate and inspiring other athletes to speak out.

Phelps ate approximately 12,000 calories per day during his intensive training days.

#2

IAN THORPE, "THE THORPEDO"

BORN OCTOBER 13, 1982 IN SYDNEY, NEW SOUTH WALES, AUSTRALIA.

Ian Thorpe has won five Olympic gold medals, three in Sydney in 2000 and two in Athens in 2004. In total, Thorpe has 11 world championship titles and has set 13 world records during his career. His specialty lay in the 200m and 400m freestyle events, where he dominated for much of his career.

LIGHTNING FROM THE ANTIPODES

Ian Thorpe is famous for his combination of size, power and technique. His ability to maintain a high cadence while maintaining impressive arm length has made him a formidable opponent. But what really set him apart was his fluid, almost effortless swimming style, which contrasted with his imposing stature.

Ian Thorpe exploded onto the international scene at just 15 years old, winning his first world championships in 1998. In Sydney in 2000, he became a national hero by winning three gold medals on home soil. However, after the Athens Games in 2004, Thorpe took an indefinite break from swimming, before announcing his retirement in 2006 at just 24 years old. In 2011, he attempted a comeback for the 2012 London Games but failed to qualify. Outside of the pool, Thorpe has been open about his mental health struggles, becoming a vocal advocate for the cause and using his platform to raise awareness.

Ian Thorpe faced doping accusations, notably before the 2000 Games. Although he tested positive in 2006, the investigation was dropped due to lack of evidence.

#3

KATIE LEDECKY
"CAPTAIN AMERICA"

BORN MARCH 17, 1997 IN WASHINGTON D.C., UNITED STATES

Katie Ledecky holds several world records, mainly in distance events. His medal collection includes numerous Olympic and world championship titles, particularly in the 400m, 800m and 1500m freestyle events.

THE EMPRESS OF THE DEEP WATERS

What sets Ledecky apart is her ability to not only dominate the long-distance events, but also be competitive in the shorter events. She possesses a rare combination of speed and endurance. Such is her dominance that she has often beaten her opponents by impressive margins, sometimes by more than 10 seconds in events like the 800m freestyle.

Upon his Olympic debut in London in 2012, Ledecky surprised the world by winning gold in the 800m freestyle at the age of 15. In 2016, at the Rio Olympics, she became the first woman since 1968 to win the 200m, 400m and 800m freestyle in a single Olympics. In addition to her Olympic prowess, she consistently pushed boundaries by setting multiple world records, solidifying her place among the greatest swimmers of all time. Out of the pool, Ledecky also impressed with his humility and dedication to his studies, pursuing an education at Stanford University while continuing to compete at the highest level.

She refused to give up on her studies despite her intense sports schedule and even managed to graduate from Stanford.

#4

MARK SPITZ, "MARK THE SHARK"

BORN FEBRUARY 10, 1950 IN MODESTO, CALIFORNIA, UNITED STATES.

Mark Spitz won seven gold medals, a record that stood until Michael Phelps surpassed it in 2008. Each of these Olympic victories was also a new world record. In total, Spitz won nine Olympic gold medals, one silver and one bronze during his appearances at the 1968 and 1972 Games.

THE GOLDEN ICON OF THE 70S

Mark Spitz is famous not only for his dominance in swimming, but also for the way he revolutionized the sport. His feat at the 1972 Olympics is one of the most iconic moments in Olympic history. With his seven gold medals, Spitz set a new standard for excellence in swimming, proving that versatility and dominance in multiple events was possible.

Mark Spitz's career hasn't always been easy. Although a promising young swimmer, he faced initial disappointments, notably at the 1968 Olympics in Mexico, where he predicted he would win six gold medals but only achieved two. This experience served as a catalyst for Spitz, pushing him to train harder and focus on Munich 1972. There, he surpassed all expectations, winning seven gold medals. His achievement was also overshadowed by the tragic Munich massacre, in which eleven members of the Israeli Olympic team were taken hostage and killed by a terrorist group. Spitz, being Jewish, was placed under enhanced protection after his victories.

Spitz almost didn't swim in 1972 because of his mustache, considered an aerodynamic disadvantage. But after setting records with it, it became a trend among swimmers.

#5

JENNY THOMPSON, "GOLDEN JENNY"

BORN FEBRUARY 26, 1973 IN DANVERS, MASSACHUSETTS, UNITED STATES.

Throughout her career, she won 12 Olympic medals, including 8 gold, 3 silver and 1 bronze. She also shone at the World Championships, winning several individual and relay gold medals. She holds the record for the highest Olympic medal winner among American swimmers until 2020.

A BURNING TALENT IN COLD WATERS

Jenny Thompson is famous for her immense swimming talent and endurance. She is often recognized for her remarkable ability to excel in relay events, adding an invaluable dynamic to the American team. She also stood out for her commitment outside the pool, pursuing a career in medicine.

Jenny Thompson began to shine early in her career, capturing attention at the Junior Nationals. But it was the Olympics that propelled her into the spotlight. One of the most iconic moments of her career came at the 2000 Sydney Olympics, where she helped break the world record in the 4x100m freestyle relay. Beyond her athletic career, Jenny also pursued medical studies and became an anesthesiologist. Her dedication to both sports and medicine shows her passion and determination to excel in everything she does.

In addition to being an Olympic swimmer, Jenny is also a medical anesthesiologist.

#6

KRISTIN OTTO
"THE MERMAID OF THE EAST"

BORN FEBRUARY 7, 1966 IN LEIPZIG, EAST GERMANY.

Kristin Otto is an exceptional swimmer who holds the record for being the first woman to win six gold medals in a single Olympic Games, a feat achieved in Seoul in 1988. These victories spanned all disciplines, backstroke freestyle swimming and relays.

THE UNDISPUTED QUEEN OF SEOUL

Kristin Otto is internationally recognized for her unique feat at the 1988 Seoul Olympics. She dominated the pool, winning six gold medals, a record for a swimmer. His versatile talent has allowed him to triumph in a variety of disciplines, demonstrating his versatility and determination.

Kristin Otto's career is marked by her dominance in Seoul, but there are other notable elements. Raised in East Germany's rigorous sporting system, she had to overcome many obstacles, including injuries that nearly ended her career before it even began. Following a serious injury in 1982, there were fears that she would never be able to compete at a high level. However, she proved those fears unfounded by coming back stronger than ever. After her stunning performance in Seoul, she retired in 1989. She later became a sports journalist, covering swimming in particular. She also became a critic of East Germany's doping system, although she always denied using banned substances.

After her retirement, Otto became a respected sports journalist in Germany.

#7

RYAN LOCHTE, "REEZY"

BORN ON AUGUST 3, 1984 IN ROCHESTER, NEW YORK, UNITED STATES.

Ryan Lochte has 12 Olympic medals to his name, including six gold, three silver and three bronze. His successes span four Olympic Games, from 2004 to 2016. Lochte has also won numerous medals at the World Championships, including being the first man to break the world record in the short course 200m backstroke.

THE SILENT FORCE BEHIND PHELPS

While Michael Phelps is often considered the face of American swimming, Ryan Lochte isn't far behind in terms of accomplishments. What sets Lochte apart is his remarkable versatility, performing at a high level in several styles. His friendly rivalry with Phelps was one of swimming's greatest duels, pushing both swimmers to exceptional performances.

Although his swimming career has been peppered with success, Lochte has also been a controversial figure outside of the pool. The most notorious incident took place during the 2016 Rio Olympics, where he and three other American swimmers claimed they were robbed at gunpoint, a claim that turned out to be false. This event led to a suspension and tarnished his reputation. Despite this controversy, Lochte returned to compete at the 2021 Olympic Trials, showing his resilience and determination to persevere in the face of adversity. He has also appeared on several reality TV shows, including "Dancing with the Stars," showcasing his larger-than-life personality.

Lochte invented his own word, "Jeah!", which he uses frequently.

#8

ALEXANDER POPOV
"THE SPRINT TSAR"

BORN NOVEMBER 16, 1971 IN SVERDLOVSK (NOW YEKATERINBURG), RUSSIA.

Olympic champion in 50m and 100m freestyle at the 1992 Summer Games in Barcelona, he repeated this feat at the Atlanta Games in 1996. In addition, he won numerous world and European medals throughout his career, reinforcing his status as one of the icons of sprint swimming.

THE SPRINT STAR

Alexander Popov's greatness lies in his ability to dominate sprint swimming for almost a decade. His swimming technique was often praised for its fluidity and simplicity, making him incredibly effective in the water. His back-to-back Olympic Games victories in 1992 and 1996 cemented his reputation as one of the greatest sprinters of all time.

In addition to his Olympic prowess, Popov's career has been punctuated by numerous highlights. He remained undefeated for seven consecutive years in the 100m freestyle at an international level. In 1994, despite being stabbed in Moscow, he miraculously recovered and continued to dominate the world stage. This resilience not only shows her determination to overcome personal obstacles, but also her unwavering passion for swimming. After retiring, he became an influential administrator in the world of swimming, highlighting his continued dedication to the sport.

Despite a knife attack in 1994, Alexander was able to return to competition triumphantly.

#9

DAWN FRASER

BORN SEPTEMBER 4, 1937 IN BALMAIN, SYDNEY, AUSTRALIA.

Dawn Fraser won eight Olympic medals, including four gold, between 1956 and 1964. She dominated the 100m freestyle, winning gold in three consecutive Olympic Games. Additionally, she set 39 world records during her career. She is also the first woman to swim the 100m freestyle in less than a minute.

SPRINT TRIPLE CROWN

Fraser is famous for her dominance of the 100m freestyle, a feat she accomplished in three consecutive Olympic editions. This unparalleled triumph, combined with her daring personality and dedication to the sport, made her one of the greatest swimmers in history. Her powerful style and fluid technique set her apart from her opponents.

Beyond his sporting achievements, Fraser has also been at the center of numerous controversies. After her victory at the 1964 Tokyo Olympics, she was accused of stealing an Olympic flag, although she denied the allegations. This controversy, combined with other behavior deemed inappropriate, earned him a suspension by the Australian Swimming Federation, ending his Olympic career. However, despite these obstacles, she has always been a beloved figure in Australia and is considered a true trailblazer for female athletes.

Fraser attempted a career in politics, becoming a member of the New South Wales Parliament.

#10

INGE DE BRUIJN
"FLYING DUTCHWOMAN"

BORN AUGUST 24, 1973 IN BARENDRECHT, NETHERLANDS.

During her distinguished career, she won a total of eight Olympic medals, including four gold. Her success came at the 2000 Sydney Olympics, where she won three gold medals by setting world records in each of these events: 50m freestyle, 100m freestyle and 100m butterfly.

THE RISE OF THE DUTCH STAR

Inge de Bruijn's fame is intrinsically linked to her phenomenal performances in Sydney. Her exploits propelled her to the international spotlight, and she became an inspiration to many aspiring swimmers. His ability to set world records in events as short as the 50m and 100m freestyle demonstrated a rare combination of speed and endurance.

Inge had a difficult time in the mid-1990s, where she had temporarily retired from competitive sport. However, her resilience and determination saw her come back strong in the late 1990s, culminating in her performances in Sydney. She continued to shine at the 2004 Athens Olympics, adding another gold medal to her collection in the 50m freestyle. Outside of the pool, she appeared on Dutch television shows, cementing her stardom in her native country.

The Dutch swimmer announced her retirement from sport on March 12, 2007 at the age of 33.

#11

PIETER VAN DEN HOOGENBAND
"HOOGIE"

BORN MARCH 14, 1978 IN MAASTRICHT, NETHERLANDS.

Pieter van den Hoogenband has won three Olympic gold medals, two at the Sydney Games in 2000 in the 100m and 200m freestyle, and another in the 100m freestyle in Athens in 2004. He also holds several European and world titles, thus solidifying his place among the greatest swimmers in history.

THE DUTCH GOLDEN RELAY

Hoogenband is famous for his dazzling performances at the 2000 Sydney Olympics, where he challenged and beat Australian Ian Thorpe on home soil in the 200m freestyle, and also broke the world record in the 100m freestyle. His ability to excel in two such different distances is a testament to his versatility and endurance, a rare combination in high-level swimming.

Hoogenband remained at the top of swimming for a decade, winning world and European titles. But it was his epic duels with the other great swimmers of his time, such as the Australian Ian Thorpe and the Russian Alexander Popov, which left their mark. These rivalries have given the swimming world some of its most memorable moments. Outside of the pool, Pieter played a crucial role as an ambassador for swimming, helping to popularize the sport in the Netherlands, a country traditionally focused on speed skating.

Victim of a herniated disc, the swimmer withdrew from the world championships in Montreal. After a long convalescence due to the operation he underwent to treat his hernia, the Dutchman returned to competition in 2006 during the European Championships in Budapest.

#12

MISSY FRANKLINN
"MISSY THE MISSILE"

BORN ON MAY 10, 1995 IN PASADENA, CALIFORNIA, UNITED STATES.

With five Olympic medals, including four gold at the London Games in 2012, Missy Franklin has established herself as one of the dominant figures in women's swimming. Add a total of sixteen world medals, including eleven gold, collected during the world championships, and you obtain one of the most impressive records in the world of swimming.

THE FRANKLIN PHENOMENON

What makes Missy Franklin unique, aside from her undeniable talent in the pool, is how quickly she rose to the top. At just 17 years old, during the London 2012 Olympic Games, she won four gold medals, setting a new world record in the 200m backstroke. Her impressive height of 1.87m, combined with impeccable arm span and technique, made her almost invincible in the water.

Missy's precociousness was breathtaking. At age 13, she competed in her first Olympic trials, and although she did not qualify, the experience prepared her for what came next. At the London 2012 Games, she became the first American woman to win four gold medals in swimming at a single Games. But Missy's road hasn't always been easy. After a disappointing performance at the 2016 Rio Games, where she won just one medal, she revealed she was battling depression. Despite these challenges, she remained an inspiration to many swimmers and used her platform to raise awareness about the importance of mental health.

At just 16 years old, at the 2011 World Swimming Championships in Shanghai, Missy Franklin set a new world record in the 4x100m medley relay, helping lead the American team to victory.

#13

NATALIE COUGHLIN

BORN ON AUGUST 23, 1982 IN VALLEJO, CALIFORNIA, UNITED STATES.

Natalie Coughlin is an American swimming icon. Throughout her career, she won 12 Olympic medals, including 3 gold, 4 silver and 5 bronze medals. Coughlin is also the first woman to successfully defend her Olympic 100m backstroke title, which she achieved at the 2008 Beijing Games.

THE VERSATILE STAR OF THE POOL

Natalie Coughlin is famous for her exceptional versatility in swimming, having shone in the backstroke, front crawl and individual events. Her innovative techniques, particularly her ability to stay underwater after starting, set her apart and put her ahead of her time. Her endurance and ability to perform at a high level over a long period of time makes her unique.

In 2008 at the Beijing Olympics, Coughlin made history by becoming the first American woman to win six medals in a single Games. Additionally, at the 2004 Athens Games, she became the first woman to swim the 100m backstroke in less than a minute. Outside of the pool, Coughlin is also an avid cook and has even appeared on the Food Network show "Chopped," demonstrating her culinary talent.

Natalie Coughlin competed on "Dancing with the Stars", reaching the 10th week of competition.

#14

MATTHEW BIONDI
"MORAGA'S TORPEDO"

BORN OCTOBER 8, 1965 IN MORAGA, CALIFORNIA, UNITED STATES.

With an impressive total of 11 Olympic medals - including 8 gold - won across three editions of the Games, Biondi has established himself as a true swimming icon. At the 1988 Seoul Olympics, he won five gold medals, setting new world records in four of those events.

THE FLIGHT OF THE "CALIFORNIA CONDOR"

Matt Biondi is famous for his lightning speed in the water and impressive wingspan, earning him the nickname "California Condor." His versatility in different events and his endurance made him one of the most dominant swimmers of his era. At the 1988 Olympic Games in Seoul, he made history by rivaling the record of seven gold medals in a single Olympics, set by Mark Spitz.

Matt Biondi is best known for his exploits in Seoul in 1988, but his journey goes well beyond that. After winning his first gold medal at the 1984 Los Angeles Olympics, Biondi made swimming history with his incredible performance in Seoul. He dominated events such as the 100m freestyle and 50m freestyle, breaking world records and establishing himself as the fastest swimmer on the planet. However, his career has not been without challenges. At the 1988 U.S. Olympic Trials, he was beaten in the 200m freestyle, a defeat that motivated him to excel in Seoul. Following his retirement from sports, Biondi engaged in teaching, demonstrating his passion for educating and encouraging the next generation.

It was through his father, a former water polo player and swimming coach, that he discovered the sport at the age of five.

#15

LIBBY TRICKETT

BORN JANUARY 28, 1985 IN TOWNSVILLE, AUSTRALIA.

Libby Trickett has won a total of four Olympic gold medals, four silver medals and three bronze medals. In addition to her Olympic success, Trickett captured eight gold medals at the World Swimming Championships, cementing her place as one of the best female swimming sprinters of all time.

AUSTRALIAN GOLD SHARD

Libby Trickett is famous not only for her dazzling speed in the water, but also for her perseverance and ability to come back after tough times. She set several world records during her career, notably in the 100 meter freestyle. Her friendly rivalry with German swimmer Britta Steffen was one of the highlights of world swimming, providing memorable races for fans around the world.

Libby's career has not been without its ups and downs. After the 2008 Beijing Olympics, she decided to take a break from swimming, but returned in 2010 with renewed determination. Unfortunately, she was unable to qualify for the individual events at the 2012 London Olympics, but still helped the Australian team secure bronze in the 4x100m freestyle relay. Outside of the pool, Libby has been committed to mental health, opening up about her own challenges with depression and anxiety to help others talk and seek help.

Libby Trickett swam against a racehorse in a promotional event in 2009, testing her speed in the water against the horse's speed on land!

#16

GRANT HACKETT
"THE COLOSSUS OF SOUTHPORT"

BORN MAY 9, 1980 IN SOUTHPORT, QUEENSLAND, AUSTRALIA.

Grant Hackett won Olympic gold in the 1500 meter freestyle at the 2000 Sydney and 2004 Athens Games, becoming the first man to successfully defend the Olympic title. He also holds 10 long course world titles and has set several world records during his career.

THE COLOSSUS OF THE DEEP

Grant Hackett is famous not only for his prowess in the pool, but also for his ability to dominate long-distance freestyle swimming for almost a decade. His resilience, endurance and ability to excel over a range of distances made him a swimming icon. His rivalry with other swimmers, notably fellow Australian Ian Thorpe, captivated the attention of the sporting world.

Grant Hackett is an example of longevity in sport. After retiring in 2008, he made a notable comeback in 2015 in an attempt to qualify for the 2016 Rio Olympics. Although he failed to secure an Olympic berth, his return to competition at the age of 35 was hailed as a testament to his determination and dedication to the sport. Outside of the pool, Hackett also had some tough times, including personal and mental health issues. However, he has worked to raise awareness of these issues and support others facing similar challenges.

Hackett once lost an arm wrestling match to Prince William during a royal visit to Australia.

#17

KRISZTINA EGERSZEGI
"THE LITTLE MERMAID OF BUDAPEST"

BORN AUGUST 16, 1974 IN BUDAPEST, HUNGARY.

Krisztina Egerszegi has won five Olympic gold medals. She excelled particularly in the backstroke events, consecutively winning the 200m backstroke at the 1988, 1992 and 1996 Olympic Games. With this performance, she became the first woman to win the same aquatic event in three consecutive Olympics.

THE RISING STAR OF THE DEEP WATERS

Egerszegi is famous for his incredible swimming talent, particularly in the backstroke events. Despite her rather small stature, she dominated the world stage for almost a decade. Her impeccable technique and incredible mental strength set her apart from other swimmers. She is also known for being one of the few swimmers to win five Olympic gold medals before the age of 22.

Krisztina Egerszegi started swimming at the tender age of 4 and quickly rose through the ranks. Her first Olympic gold medal at the age of 14 at the 1988 Seoul Games came as a surprise to many, but it was only the beginning. In addition to her Olympic medals, she has also won numerous world and European championships. Her dominance in the backstroke events put her in competition with the best swimmers of her era, but she often had the upper hand thanks to her determination and hard training. She also served as the flag bearer for Hungary during the opening ceremonies of the Olympic Games, underscoring her status as one of the country's greatest sportswomen.

Although a competitive swimmer, Egerszegi was afraid of water as a child.

#18

DEBBIE MEYER

BORN AUGUST 14, 1952 IN ANNAPOLIS, MARYLAND, UNITED STATES.

Debbie Meyer is best known for being the first swimmer to win three individual gold medals in a single Olympic Games. This remarkable feat was achieved at the 1968 Mexico Games, where she dominated the 200m, 400m and 800m freestyle events.

THE "TRIPLE CROWN" OF MEXICO

She became the first swimmer to win three individual events – a feat that earned her a place in Olympic history. Her victories not only set new standards for women's swimming, but also inspired future generations of swimmers.

Meyer started swimming at a young age and quickly rose through the ranks to become a world-class swimmer. Under the guidance of her coach Sherman Chavoor, she developed technique and endurance that propelled her to the top of world swimming. In addition to her Olympic medals, she set 15 world records throughout her career. After retiring from competition, Meyer remained involved in the swimming world as a coach and advocate for swimming for all.

At the age of 16, before her historic performance at the Olympics, Debbie had an emergency appendectomy. She recovered quickly and continued to dominate the pool.

#19

MURRAY ROSE, "SEAWEED STREAK"

BORN JANUARY 6, 1939 IN BIRMINGHAM, ENGLAND.

During her career, Rose won six Olympic medals, including four gold. At the 1956 Melbourne Olympics, at the age of 17, he won three gold medals: in the 400m, 1500m freestyle and in the 4x200m relay. He added another gold medal in the 400m freestyle at the 1960 Rome Games.

THE AUSTRALIAN NAVY STAR

Murray Rose is celebrated for being the first man to swim the 1500m in under 18 minutes. His dominance in long distance freestyle swimming in the 1950s and early 1960s made him a key figure in the world of swimming. Rose's impact on the sport goes far beyond medals; he is also known for his holistic approach to training and his vegetarian diet, which was quite rare at the time for a top athlete.

Murray Rose's career has had many memorable moments, but his performance at the 1956 Melbourne Olympics is particularly iconic. At the age of 17, he became the nation's hero by winning three gold medals, solidifying his place as one of the greatest Australian swimmers of all time. Outside of the pool, Rose was also known for his commitment to charitable causes and his passion for theater and cinema, having appeared in several films.

Murray Rose was a staunch vegetarian and attributed his fitness to his diet.

#20

KIEREN PERKINS

BORN AUGUST 14, 1973 IN BRISBANE, QUEENSLAND, AUSTRALIA.

Perkins won Olympic gold in the 1500 meter freestyle event in 1992 in Barcelona and 1996 in Atlanta. He also won silver in the same event at the 2000 Sydney Games. Perkins has also been crowned world champion several times and has broken numerous world records.

THE GOLD OF THE BOTTOM

Kieren Perkins is famous for dominating the international long-distance freestyle swimming scene during the 1990s. His ability to maintain a high, consistent cadence during long-distance races set him apart from his competitors. His perseverance, determination and love of competition elevated him to the status of an Australian swimming legend.

Perkins amazed the world when he won gold in Barcelona in 1992, setting a new Olympic record. In Atlanta in 1996, although he qualified with difficulty for the 1500m final, he surprised everyone by winning gold from the least favorable lane. The triumph was hailed as one of the greatest comebacks in Olympic history. Out of the pool, Perkins is also known for his leadership, having captained the Australian swimming team. Following his retirement from sport, he continued to influence sport in Australia, holding various administrative positions, including within Swimming Australia.

Despite qualifying in eighth position for the Olympic 1500m final in Atlanta in 1996, Kieren Perkins managed to win gold.

#21

PETER THOMAS

BORN AUGUST 25, 1975 IN LISMORE, NEW SOUTH WALES, AUSTRALIA.

During her impressive career, she won three Olympic gold medals, all at the 2004 Athens Games. She bagged eight world championship medals, including gold in the 200m butterfly in 1998 and 2001. In addition to this, Thomas collected 13 Commonwealth Games medals across three different editions.

WINGED TRIUMPH: THE RISE OF A BUTTERFLY RIDER

Petria Thomas distinguished herself primarily in the butterfly events, where she often challenged and overcame world competition. Her victories in Athens in 2004 are all the more remarkable given that she had already undergone three shoulder operations and one wrist operation before these Games. Her dedication, resilience and ability to come back stronger after challenges make her career a true source of inspiration.

Thomas' career is as much a story of sporting triumph as it is of determination in the face of adversity. Before her Olympic victories, she underwent no fewer than three major shoulder operations, putting her career in jeopardy each time. Each surgery was challenging, both physically and mentally. Yet with an unwavering spirit, Thomas came back every time, proving that perseverance can overcome even the greatest obstacles. In addition to the physical challenges, she has also spoken openly about her struggles with depression, shedding light on the importance of mental health in sport.

Underwent shoulder surgery more than three times while continuing to excel.

#22

CAESAR SKY

ON JANUARY 10, 1987, IN SANTA BÁRBARA D'OESTE, SÃO PAULO, BRÉSIL.

César Cielo distinguished himself on the international scene by winning gold in the 50m freestyle at the Beijing Olympic Games in 2008. In addition to this Olympic gold medal, Cielo was world champion on several occasions, notably in the 50m and 100m freestyle swimming, as well as 50m butterfly.

A BRAZILIAN IN THE SPRINTER FIRMAMENT

Brazilian swimming found its star in the person of César Cielo. By becoming the first Brazilian swimmer to win an Olympic gold medal in freestyle, he set a new standard for his country. His explosive style and impeccable technique allowed him to dominate sprint events for several years, making him one of the most feared swimmers of his generation.

Cielo is not just a champion: he is a record breaker. In 2009, at the World Championships in Rome, he set world records in the 50m and 100m freestyle. These performances were all the more impressive because he managed to break these records in polyurethane suits, which were later banned. His ability to push the boundaries of what is possible in swimming has inspired a new generation of Brazilian swimmers to pursue excellence.

In 2023, Cielo was inducted into the International Swimming Hall of Fame.

#23

TRACY CAULKINS

BORN JANUARY 11, 1963 IN WINONA, MINNESOTA, UNITED STATES.

Tracy Caulkins won three Olympic gold medals at the 1984 Los Angeles Games, dominating the 200m medley, 400m medley and 4x100m medley. She was also a world champion and set several world and national records, accumulating 48 national titles across all swimming disciplines, an unrivaled record.

THE SWIMMING POOL CHAMELEON

Tracy Caulkins is famous for her exceptional versatility in the pool. She is the only swimmer in history to hold American records in every swimming event, affirming her position as one of the most versatile swimmers of all time. His prowess in multiple disciplines has earned him the recognition and admiration not only of his compatriots but also of the international swimming community.

Tracy Caulkins was on the rise in the 1970s and was likely to shine at the 1980 Olympics. However, the American boycott of the 1980 Moscow Games put a damper on her Olympic rise. Despite this disappointment, Caulkins never let this setback affect his passion and determination. She came back strong, winning three gold medals at the 1984 Olympics in Los Angeles. Her ability to excel in all swimming disciplines, from sprint events to longer distances, to all strokes, marks her out as a true swimming legend. She also played a key role in the development and promotion of women's swimming in the United States.

Aside from her swimming career, Tracy Caulkins was an outstanding student, having been named the NCAA Student-Athlete of the Year twice.

#24

MARY T. MEAGHER
"MRS. BUTTERFLY"

BORN OCTOBER 27, 1964 IN LOUISVILLE, KENTUCKY, UNITED STATES

Mary T. Meagher won three gold medals at the 1984 Olympic Games in Los Angeles: 100m butterfly, 200m butterfly and the 4x100m medley relay. She was also a multiple world champion and set several world records during her career.

BUTTERFLY QUEEN

Mary T. Meagher is primarily famous for her dominance in butterfly events. Her nickname, "Madame Butterfly", is proof of her unparalleled talent in this discipline. She set world records at the age of just 16, which stood for almost two decades, a feat rarely seen in the sporting world.

In 1981, at the age of 16, Mary set world records for the 100m and 200m butterfly at the US Championships, times so fast that they were not broken until 1999 and 2000 respectively. Unfortunately, due to the United States' boycott of the 1980 Olympics, she did not have the opportunity to turn those performances into Olympic medals that year. However, she made up for this by winning three gold medals at the 1984 Games. Outside of the swimming pools, Mary is also recognized for her grace and humility, she is often cited as a role model for young swimmers.

She set a world record at the age of 16 that stood for 19 years!

#25

PENNY OLEKSIAK

BORN JUNE 13, 2000 IN TORONTO, CANADA.

Penny Oleksiak emerged as a swimming sensation during the 2016 Rio Olympics at just 16 years old. She won four medals, including gold in the 100m butterfly, becoming the first Canadian to win four medals in a single Olympic edition.

PRODIGY OF THE PONDS

Penny Oleksiak is famous not only for her incredible aquatic performances, but also for how quickly she rose to the top of world swimming. His versatility and ability to excel in different swimming strokes, including freestyle and butterfly, stunned the sporting community.

Penny's career has been marked by a meteoric rise. At the 2016 Olympic Games, she not only won four medals, but also set a new Olympic record in the 100m butterfly. His success at such a young age highlighted the depth of Canadian swimming talent and solidified his position as one of swimming's rising stars. Outside of the pool, Penny has become a role model for young swimmers, emphasizing the importance of perseverance and hard work.

Penny is the younger sister of NHL ice hockey player Jamie Oleksiak.

#26

SHANE GOULD

BORN NOVEMBER 23, 1956 IN SYDNEY, AUSTRALIA.

At the 1972 Munich Olympics, she won three gold medals, a silver and a bronze, all before the age of 16. She also holds the distinctive record of having been, at one time, the world record holder for all freestyle distances, from 100m to 1500m.

SHOOTING STAR OF THE POOLS

Shane Gould is primarily famous for his explosion onto the swimming scene at an incredibly young age. By 1972, she was arguably the most dominant swimmer in the world, with a versatility that allowed her to set world records over multiple distances. His career, although short, left an indelible mark on the history of sport.

The year 1972 was the high point of Gould's career. At the Munich Olympics, she became the first woman to win three individual gold medals in a single Olympic edition. After those games, Gould shocked the swimming world by retiring at the age of just 16, making her one of the most brilliant and short-lived sports stars of all time. Later in life, she returned to education, studied photography and became a swimming coach, sharing her passion and expertise with subsequent generations.

Shane Gould, after dominating the global swimming scene and winning numerous medals and world records, made the unexpected choice to retire from competition at the age of 16.

#27

FRANZISKA VANALMSICK

BORN APRIL 5, 1978 IN BERLIN, GERMANY.

Franziska Van Almsick won two silver medals and two bronze medals at the 1992 Olympic Games in Barcelona at just 14 years old. She added a silver and a bronze medal at the 1996 Games in Atlanta. Franzi won a total of ten world championship medals and numerous European titles.

THE LUMINOUS ASCENSION AND THE ASTONISHING QUEST FOR GOLD BY FRANZISKA VAN ALMSICK

Franziska Van Almsick is famous for her precocious talent, having burst onto the international scene as a teenager. Her impressive performances at the 1992 Barcelona Olympics made her a national sensation in Germany. His specialty was crawl and 200m freestyle.

Franzi became a national phenomenon after Barcelona, with intense pressure to continue succeeding. Unfortunately, at the 2000 Sydney and 2004 Athens Games, she failed to medal, which was disappointing for many. However, his resilience and determination to persevere despite hardships are an integral part of his legacy. She retired after the Athens Games, but her impact on German swimming remains indelible. She was also an ambassador for the sport, using her fame to promote swimming in Germany.

Franzi has his own perfume brand called "Franzi".

#28

IAN CROCKER

BORN AUGUST 31, 1982 IN PORTLAND, MAINE, UNITED STATES.

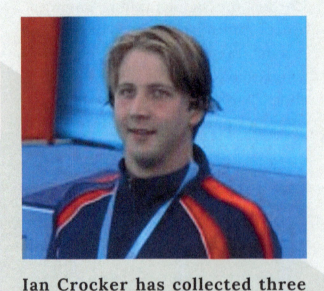

Ian Crocker has collected three Olympic gold medals, all in relay events. At the 2004 Athens Olympics, he set a world record in the 100m butterfly, although he ultimately won silver behind compatriot Michael Phelps. Additionally, Crocker was a five-time world champion.

AMERICAN BUTTERFLY EAGLE

Ian Crocker is famous for his exploits in the butterfly discipline. During the 2000s, he was one of the few swimmers to seriously compete with Michael Phelps in this discipline. His powerful swimming style and ability to produce explosive finishes earned him the nickname "The Rocket". The rivalry between Crocker and Phelps, particularly in the 100m butterfly.

Ian Crocker's career was marked by his fierce competition with Michael Phelps. One of the most memorable moments was during the 2004 Olympic Games in Athens. While Crocker broke the world record in the 100m butterfly semifinals, Phelps narrowly surpassed him in the final, relegating him to second place. Despite the loss, Crocker played a vital role in the 4x100m medley relay, helping the American team win gold and set a new world record. Outside of the pool, Crocker is also a musician and has even played in a rock band, providing an extra dimension to his personality.

Ian Crocker is also a guitarist in a rock band.

#29

STEPHANIE RICE

BORN JUNE 17, 1988 IN BRISBANE, QUEENSLAND, AUSTRALIA.

Triple Olympic champion, Stephanie Rice marked the 2008 Beijing Olympic Games by winning three gold medals: 200m individual medley, 400m individual medley and 4x200m freestyle. During these victories, she set world records in each of these events.

THE QUEEN OF THE FOUR SWIMMING POOLS OF BEIJING

Stephanie Rice is best known for her outstanding performances at the 2008 Beijing Olympics. Her ability to master all four strokes made her a dominant competitor in the medley events. Her victories, combined with her world records, catapulted her to national stardom in Australia and earned her international recognition.

Beyond her exploits in the pool, Stephanie Rice's life has been scrutinized due to her popularity. After Beijing, she became a celebrity in Australia, appearing on several television shows, including the Australian version of "Dancing with the Stars." However, her swimming career was hampered by shoulder injuries, prompting her to retire at the age of 24 in 2014. Despite this untimely end, Rice remains one of the most accomplished and beloved female swimmers from Australia.

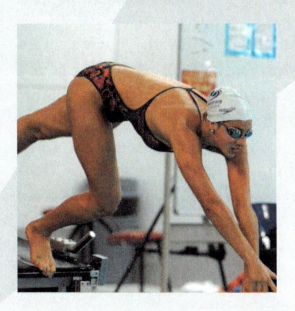

In addition to her successful swimming career, Stephanie Rice has demonstrated her entrepreneurial flair by launching her own swimwear line called "RICE."

#30

AMANDA BEARD

BORN ON OCTOBER 29, 1981 IN NEWPORT BEACH, CALIFORNIA, UNITED STATES.

Amanda Beard, with an impressive total of seven Olympic medals (2 gold, 4 silver, 1 bronze) won over three editions of the Olympic Games (1996, 2000, 2004), her determination and talent are undeniable. She is particularly famous for her victories in the breaststroke and 4x100 meter medley relay.

90S AQUATIC WONDER

Amanda Beard became a phenomenon at a young age. She entered the Olympic stage at the tender age of 14 during the 1996 Games in Atlanta, where she captured the hearts of Americans not only with her medals, but also by taking her beloved teddy bear to the podium. Her youth coupled with her precocious talent made her one of the rising stars of American swimming.

In addition to her impressive athletic record, Amanda Beard's life has been marked by personal challenges outside the pool. She has spoken openly about her struggles with depression, drug addiction and eating disorders. By sharing her experiences, she has become an inspiration to many, demonstrating that mental challenges can affect anyone, even world-class athletes. Her autobiography, "In the Water They Can't See You Cry," details these struggles and how she was able to overcome them.

At the 1996 Atlanta Olympics, 14-year-old Amanda Beard became famous not only for her incredible performances in the pool, but also for taking her teddy bear, named "Harley," to the podium. with her.

#31

REBECCA ADLINGTON

BORN ON FEBRUARY 17, 1989 IN MANSFIELD, ENGLAND, UNITED KINGDOM.

Rebecca Adlington won two gold medals at the 2008 Beijing Olympics, in the 400m and 800m freestyle events. Four years later, at the London Games, she added two bronze medals to her collection in the same events. During her career, she also won several European and world titles.

THE MANSFIELD MERMAID

Rebecca Adlington emerged as a beacon of hope for British swimming when she claimed two gold medals in Beijing. Her victory in the 800m freestyle, where she broke the world record, catapulted her to national superstardom. Known for her smooth technique and determination, she is often hailed for revitalizing interest in swimming in the UK.

Following her victories in Beijing, Rebecca became an icon of British sport. Her gold medals were the first for a British woman in swimming since 1960. In London, despite the enormous pressure of swimming at home, she managed to secure two bronze medals. Outside of the pool, Adlington has always been a strong advocate for sport and mental health. In 2013, she founded Rebecca Adlington SwimStars, an initiative to help children learn to swim and promote the importance of water safety.

she became a member of the International Swimming Hall of Fame in 2018

#32

AARON PEIRSOL
"THE BACKSTROKE KING"

BORN ON JULY 23, 1983 IN IRVINE, CALIFORNIA, UNITED STATES.

Aaron Peirsol has won five Olympic gold medals over the course, with three titles at the Athens Olympics in 2004 and two in Beijing in 2008. He holds several world records in the backstroke, both in the short course and long course. Peirsol also won numerous titles throughout his career.

THE MASTER OF TWO

Aaron Peirsol is famous for his unprecedented dominance in backstroke events. His fluid and powerful technique has propelled him to the pinnacle of his sport, allowing him to set and redefine world records repeatedly. What was particularly notable was how he managed to maintain this excellence over such a prolonged period, remaining competitive and consistently dominant on the world stage.

Beyond his impressive track record, Peirsol's commitment to protecting the oceans deserves to be highlighted. Passionate about the sea, he has partnered with various environmental organizations to raise awareness about marine conservation. One of his most notable achievements outside of the pool is his collaboration with "Oceana", an international organization focused on protecting the oceans. Peirsol has used his platform and fame to promote environmental causes, illustrating that his impact goes far beyond records and medals.

Peirsol is also an avid surfer and has even tried his luck in local surfing competitions in California.

#33

RANOMI KROMOWIDJOJO

BORN AUGUST 20, 1990 IN SAUWERD, NETHERLANDS.

At the 2012 London Olympics, Ranomi Kromowidjojo won gold in the 50m and 100m freestyle events, proving that she was the fastest swimmer in the world at that time. She also has numerous medals from the World Championships, both in short and long course.

THE QUEEN OF AQUATIC SPRINTING

Kromowidjojo's strength lies in his ability to maintain a constant speed throughout his run. Her swimming technique, her power and her mental steel have made her one of the most feared swimmers in sprint events. She is not only famous for her Olympic prowess but also for setting several world records during her career.

Ranomi's career has been punctuated by countless victories, but also challenges. After contracting meningitis in 2010, she staged an impressive comeback, eventually winning two Olympic gold medals in 2012. This triumph in the face of adversity is one of the many reasons she is so admired. Additionally, her sportsmanship and dedication to swimming have made her an iconic figure and a source of inspiration for many young swimmers around the world.

Ranomi speaks fluent Japanese, having developed a passion for Japanese culture.

#34

LAURE MANAUDOU
"THE MERMAID OF VILLEURBANNE"

BORN OCTOBER 9, 1986 IN VILLEURBANNE, FRANCE.

Laure Manaudou won gold in the 400m freestyle at the Athens Olympic Games in 2004, becoming the first French woman to win an Olympic gold medal in swimming since 1952. She has also won numerous medals at the World Championships and Europe, confirming its domination in international basins.

THE RISE OF MANAUDOU

Laure Manaudou is famous for having broken numerous records and for having restored the nobility of French swimming on the international scene. Her commitment, tenacity and passion for swimming have made her a sporting icon in France and around the world.

Laure's trajectory was not limited to her aquatic prowess. After her victories in Athens, she experienced difficult times, notably with coaching changes and media controversies. In 2007, she decided to move to the United States to train, seeking a new lease on life for her career. Despite the challenges, Laure came back strong, proving her resilience and determination. Outside of the pool, she also participated in television shows, and she moved into the world of fashion and business, showing another side of her personality.

Laure wrote an autobiographical book at the age of 22 entitled "Between the Lines".

#35

MICHAEL GROSS, "ALBATROS"

BORN JUNE 17, 1964 IN FRANKFURT AM MAIN, GERMANY

Michael Gross won a total of four Olympic gold medals, two at the 1984 Los Angeles Olympics (200m freestyle and 100m butterfly) and two at the 1988 Seoul Olympics (200m freestyle and 200m butterfly). Gross also won three world titles and set several world records.

THE ALBATROSS ELK

Michael Gross is celebrated for his exceptional swimming technique and impressive arm reach, earning him the nickname "Albatross." His dominance in the mid-1980s not only set new standards in swimming, but also propelled Germany to the forefront of the world swimming stage. His ability to excel in varied styles showed a versatility rarely seen.

Besides his Olympic medals and world titles, one of the most memorable moments of Gross's career was at the 1983 European Championships in Rome, where he broke the world record in the 200m freestyle. But more than his exploits in the water, Gross was a leading figure for German swimming at a time when the country was seeking to reassert itself on the international sporting stage after the East German doping scandal of the 1970s. Gross embodied clean competition, based on natural talent and hard work.

Nicknamed "the albatross" because of his great wingspan, he is one of the most successful swimmers in history.

#36

YANA KLOCHKOVA
"THE MERMAID OF UKRAINE"

BORN AUGUST 7, 1982 IN SIMFEROPOL, UKRAINE

With a total of four Olympic gold medals - two in Sydney in 2000 and two in Athens in 2004, all in the medley events (200m and 400m) - her reputation as an all-round specialist is well deserved. Adding to this five world titles and ten European titles, his list of achievements is one of the most extensive in world swimming.

VERSATILITY AT ITS PAROXYSM

Yana Klochkova is famous for her impressive swimming versatility. This ability to excel in a variety of styles and distances has earned him a place in the history of the sport. She not only collected medals in the medley events at the Olympics, but she also successfully defended her titles, proving her dominance and consistency.

Yana Klochkova has often been praised for her ability to handle pressure and excel when the stakes are highest. At the Sydney Olympic Games in 2000, despite being 18 years old, she dominated the medley events, creating a surprise. Four years later, in Athens, she confirmed her supremacy by defending her titles. Outside of the pool, her humble personality and commitment to excellence have made her extremely popular, not only in Ukraine but also internationally. She also played a key role in popularizing swimming in Ukraine, encouraging many young people to follow in her footsteps.

Yana started swimming to improve her health after often being ill as a child.

#37

LASZLO CSEH
"HUNGARIAN BUTTERFLY"

BORN DECEMBER 3, 1985 IN BUDAPEST, HUNGARY

Laszlo Cseh has accumulated six Olympic medals, but unfortunately none gold. At the World Swimming Championships, he won seventeen medals, including five gold. His victories at the European Championships are also impressive, with a haul of twenty-three medals, including fourteen gold.

THE TITAN STILL IN THE SHADOWS

Laszlo Cseh is famous for being one of the few swimmers who has consistently competed with titans such as Michael Phelps and Ryan Lochte. Her specialty lies in medley and butterfly events. However, despite his undeniable talents, Cseh was often overshadowed by these giants, often finishing second or third behind them in major competitions.

Laszlo Cseh has often been called "the best swimmer to never win an Olympic gold medal." His duel with Michael Phelps at the 2008 Olympic Games in Beijing was memorable. Although he finished second to Phelps in three races, he managed to break several European records. Additionally, at the 2016 European Championships, Cseh put in a spectacular performance winning four gold medals, proving once again that he was still at the top despite his advancing age. Outside of the pool, Cseh is known for his commitment to promoting swimming in Hungary, inspiring the next generation of swimmers.

Cseh has often joked about having "the most complete Olympic medal collection without gold."

#38

DARA TORRES

BORN ON APRIL 15, 1967 IN BEVERLY HILLS, CALIFORNIA, UNITED STATES.

Dara Torres is one of the most decorated swimmers in the United States. Throughout her career spanning five Olympic Games, she won 12 medals, including 4 gold, 4 silver and 4 bronze. His favorite events included freestyle and relay.

LONGEVITY AS A SIGN OF DISTINCTION

Dara Torres is primarily famous for defying age conventions in competitive sport. Not only has she competed in five Olympics, but she also became the oldest swimmer to qualify for the Olympics at age 41 in 2008. Her longevity, dedication and perseverance have made her an inspiration to many athletes and sports enthusiasts.

Dara Torres began her Olympic career in 1984 and extended until 2008. One of the most notable moments of her career was when she took a break after the 2000 Sydney Olympics, only to return then in 2008 in Beijing, proving that age was just a number. Not only did she qualify, but she also won three silver medals, narrowly missing out on gold by a split second. In addition to her athletic achievements, Dara has been an ambassador for sports, encouraging women and older athletes to push their limits and pursue their passions regardless of social conventions or expectations.

Even at 40, Torres was able to beat swimmers who were practically half her age.

#39

FLORENT MANAUDOU

BORN NOVEMBER 12, 1990 IN VILLEURBANNE, FRANCE.

Florent Manaudou won the gold medal in the 50 meter freestyle at the London 2012 Olympic Games. In addition to his Olympic success, he has won numerous world and European titles, thus strengthening his reputation as an exceptional swimmer, particularly over short distances.

THE KING OF THE FRENCH SPRINT

Florent Manaudou quickly made a name for himself in the world of swimming thanks to his explosive speed and powerful style. His talent over short distances, particularly the 50m freestyle, sets him apart. His Olympic victory in London solidified his status as one of the greatest sprint swimmers of his generation.

Manaudou surprised the swimming world when he won gold in London 2012, beating the favorites. In 2015, at the World Swimming Championships in Kazan, he demonstrated his dominance by winning three gold medals. But beyond swimming, Florent took a break to explore professional handball before returning to swimming. This return was crowned with success with a silver medal at the Rio Olympic Games in 2016. His journey, marked by challenges, comebacks and victories, made him an emblematic figure of French swimming.

Florent tried his luck in professional handball between 2016 and 2017.

#40

ADAM PEATY

BORN DECEMBER 28, 1994 IN UTTOXETER, ENGLAND.

Adam Peaty is recognized as one of the greatest brewers of all time. World record holder in the 100m breaststroke, he is the first man to swim this distance in less than 57 seconds. Olympic champion in Rio and Tokyo in the 100m breaststroke, he also won multiple gold medals at the World and European Championships.

THE UNPARALLELED BREWER

Adam Peaty is synonymous with breaststroke dominance. His ability to push the limits of what is possible in the 100m breaststroke has catapulted him to the pinnacle of his sport. His impeccable technique, combined with raw strength, sets him apart as the swimmer to beat in every competition.

Adam's rise to power has been remarkable. At the 2015 World Swimming Championships in Kazan, he broke the world record in the 100m breaststroke. But it was at the 2016 Rio Olympics that he truly came into his own, winning gold while breaking his own world record. Peaty is also the first swimmer to win seven World Championship titles over a single distance (100m breaststroke). But it's not just his speed that impresses; his consistency and ability to perform under pressure have cemented his reputation as a great competitor.

Affected by his mental health, Peaty gave up participating in the British championships in 2023 and then was not selected for the world championships.

#41

LEISEL JONES

BORN AUGUST 30, 1985 IN KATHERINE, AUSTRALIA.

Leisel Jones has won a total of nine Olympic medals, including three gold. Jones also dominated the World Swimming Championships, with seven gold medals. At the Commonwealth Games, his supremacy was demonstrated by ten gold medals. She also competed in four consecutive Olympics.

THE AUSTRALIAN BREASTSTROKE LEGEND

Leisel Jones is an iconic figure in Australian swimming, not only for his athletic prowess, but also for his longevity in a demanding sport. She distinguished herself by breaking several world records and defying expectations in every competition. His impeccable breaststroke technique has been studied by many aspiring swimmers.

Leisel Jones made history when she became the youngest Australian swimmer to compete in the Olympics at the age of 15 in 2000. But that was just the start of a meteoric career. In 2008 at the Beijing Olympics, she won gold in three different events, asserting her dominance in the breaststroke. However, beyond the pool, Jones faced personal challenges. She spoke openly about her battles with depression and intense public and media expectations, which shed light on the mental pressures faced by top athletes. Despite these obstacles, she continued to shine, becoming an inspiration to many young swimmers and highlighting the importance of mental health in sport.

She therefore equals Ian Thorpe's record and becomes with him Australia's most decorated Olympic athlete.

#42

SARAH SJÖSTRÖM, "FLY GIRL"

BORN AUGUST 17, 1993 IN SALEM, SWEDEN.

Sarah Sjöström is a butterfly, freestyle and backstroke specialist. She has won multiple gold medals at the FINA World Swimming Championships and the European Championships. At the 2016 Olympic Games in Rio, she won gold in the 100m butterfly, setting a new world record.

L'ASCENSION IMPECCABLE DE SJÖSTRÖM

Sjöström is famous not only for his speed, but also for his impeccable technique, especially in butterfly. She is the first Swedish woman to win an Olympic gold medal in swimming since 1952. Her determination and ability to push her limits has been an inspiration to many young swimmers. Additionally, her versatility, being competitive in multiple styles, shows her mastery of swimming.

In addition to her Olympic success, Sarah set several world records, including in butterfly and freestyle. In 2017, during the World Swimming Championships in Budapest, she became the first swimmer to win the 50m, 100m and 200m butterfly titles at a single world championship, thus asserting her dominance in this discipline. Outside of the pool, she has been a role model for perseverance and determination, facing injuries but always coming back stronger.

Sarah started swimming at the age of 9 after trying football and handball.

#43

KOSUKE KITAJIMA, "FROG KING"

BORN SEPTEMBER 22, 1982 IN TOKYO, JAPAN.

Kosuke Kitajima dominated breaststroke events in the early 21st century, winning back-to-back gold medals at the 2004 Athens and 2008 Beijing Olympics in the 100 and 200 meter breaststroke. He also won numerous medals at the World Championships and held several world records.

THE BREASTSTROKE ARTIST

Kosuke Kitajima is famous for redefining breaststroke, both in terms of technique and results. The first swimmer to complete the 100m-200m breaststroke double in two consecutive Olympic Games, he left an indelible mark in the history of swimming. Additionally, his intense rivalry with American swimmer Brendan Hansen captivated swimming fans around the world, each pushing the other to reach new heights.

Kitajima first came to prominence when he won both breaststroke events at the 2002 Asian Games. Two years later, he completed the Olympic double in Athens, breaking the 100m world record in the process. He then successfully defended his titles in Beijing in 2008. But it's not just Kitajima's medal collection that impresses; it's his ability to excel under pressure, often coming from behind to claim victory in the final meters. Out of the pool, Kitajima moved to the United States to train, a move that improved his technique and allowed him to compete with the world's best swimmers.

Kosuke has his own theme song, played when he steps onto the starting block during competitions in Japan.

#44

DUNCAN ARMSTRONG, "DUNKS"

BORN APRIL 7, 1968 IN ROCKHAMPTON, QUEENSLAND, AUSTRALIA.

Duncan Armstrong is best known for his phenomenal performance at the 1988 Seoul Olympics, where he won gold in the 200m freestyle and silver in the 400m freestyle. By achieving these feats, he broke the world record in the 200m freestyle.

SEOUL'S SURPRISE

Duncan Armstrong's fame rests on his ability to defy expectations. At the 1988 Seoul Olympics, he caused a surprise by beating the favorite and setting a new world record in the 200m freestyle. His iconic coach, Laurie Lawrence, played a vital role in his preparation and success, instilling a fighter mentality in Duncan.

One of the most memorable moments of Duncan Armstrong's career occurred during the 1988 Olympics. Before that competition, few would have predicted that he would beat the defending champion, American Matt Biondi, in the 200m free swim. But under the leadership of his coach Laurie Lawrence, and with unwavering determination, Duncan not only won gold, but he also set a new world record. This performance has been hailed as one of the greatest feats in Australian swimming history. Following his swimming career, Duncan also distinguished himself as a sports commentator, sharing his expertise and passion for sports with viewers around the world.

Duncan was named "Young Australian of the Year" in 1989.

#45

CHAD LE CLOS

BORN ON APRIL 12, 1992 IN DURBAN, KWAZULU-NATAL, SOUTH AFRICA.

Chad le Clos distinguished himself at the 2012 London Olympics by winning gold in the 200m butterfly, beating swimming icon Michael Phelps. Chad also won silver in the 100m butterfly at the same games. He also dominated the World Short Course and Long Course Swimming Championships.

THE MAN WHO CHALLENGED PHELPS

Chad le Clos is most famous for beating Michael Phelps, often considered the greatest swimmer of all time, at the 2012 London Olympics. This victory not only cemented his place among the elites of world swimming, but also highlighted his determination and fighting spirit.

Chad le Clos' victory against Michael Phelps in London in 2012 is arguably the most memorable moment of his career. Many considered Phelps unbeatable, especially in his favorite discipline, the 200m butterfly. However, Le Clos was able to take advantage of his mental strength and technique to create a real sensation. The emotional reaction of his father, Bert le Clos, during a post-race interview went viral, showing the world the passion and enthusiasm that surrounds swimming. Chad continued to shine, winning numerous medals at various championships, and becoming one of the most decorated swimmers at the Commonwealth Games.

Chad le Clos, along with hockey player Phumelela Mbande, was named flag bearer for the South African delegation at the 2020 Olympic Games in Tokyo.

#46

SUN YANG, "THE DISTANCE KING"

BORN DECEMBER 1, 1991 IN HANGZHOU, ZHEJIANG, CHINA.

Sun Yang, multiple Olympic champion, captivated the swimming world with his power and endurance. He won Olympic gold medals in the 400m, 800m and 1500m freestyle, setting an impressive world record in the latter distance.

THE EMPEROR OF LONG DISTANCE

Sun Yang is credited with redefining long-distance racing in swimming. Not only did he break world records, but he also introduced a new racing dynamic, combining power and tactics. His imposing stature and fluid swimming style have made him an iconic figure in Chinese swimming.

Sun Yang made history when he became the first Chinese man to win an Olympic gold medal in swimming at the London Games in 2012. However, his career has also been marked by controversies. In 2014, he was suspended for three months for doping, a fact that was revealed much later by Chinese authorities. Then, in 2018, an altercation with a controller during a doping test led to another suspension. Despite these controversies, his undeniable talent and determination have kept him in the spotlight, and he remains one of the most polarizing figures in swimming.

In 2014, he tested positive for trimetazidine, a drug used to treat angina but which was added to the World Anti-Doping Agency's list of banned substances that year.

#47

RUTA MEILUTYTE
"THE LITHUANIAN MERMAID"

BORN MARCH 19, 1997 IN KAUNAS, LITHUANIA.

Ruta Meilutyte burst onto the international scene at the 2012 Olympic Games in London, where, at just 15 years old, she won the gold medal in the 100m breaststroke, setting a new Olympic record. In addition to her Olympic achievement, Meilutyte also won several world and European titles.

THE KAUNAS COMET

Ruta Meilutyte is famous for being a true rising star in the world of swimming. Her surprise victory at the 2012 London Olympics catapulted her into the spotlight at a very young age. She has become an inspiration to many young swimmers, proving that age is just a number and that talent, coupled with determination, can lead to success.

Ruta Meilutyte, despite her young career, has had her ups and downs. After his success in London, the pressure and expectations were high. She managed to maintain a high level of performance, winning titles at the World Championships and setting world records. However, despite his success, Ruta also spoke about the mental challenges of high-performance sport. In 2019, she received a one-year suspension for missing three drug tests, although she never tested positive. It put a pause on his career, but also highlighted the challenges elite athletes face. She then took an indefinite break from swimming to focus on her mental health.

Ruta became the youngest Lithuanian Olympic champion in history at 15 years old.

#48

CAMILLE MUFFAT

BORN OCTOBER 28, 1989 IN NICE, FRANCE

At the 2012 London Olympics, she won gold in the 400m freestyle, silver in the 200m freestyle, and bronze in the 4x200m freestyle relay. She also shone at the World and European Championships, winning multiple medals.

THE SHINING STAR OF FRENCH SWIMMING

Camille Muffat made history not only for her phenomenal performances in the pool, but also for her determination and passion for swimming. She has established herself as a specialist in middle-distance freestyle swimming events. Despite a relatively short career, she left an indelible mark on the world of swimming, both through her records and her humble and dedicated personality.

Camille Muffat, although exceptional in the pool, surprised the sporting world in 2014 by announcing her retirement at the age of 24, at the peak of her form. This decision was respected, although it left his fans and peers wanting to see more. Tragically, her life was cut short when she died in a helicopter crash in Argentina in 2015 while filming a reality TV show. This sudden loss came as a shock to the sporting world and left a void in the hearts of the swimming community.

Camille could swim 100m freediving at the age of 12.

#49

OTYLIA JĘDRZEJCZAK, "OLA"

BORN DECEMBER 13, 1983 IN RUDA ŚLĄSKA, POLAND

Otylia Jędrzejczak, won the gold medal in the 200m butterfly at the 2004 Athens Olympics, also setting a new world record. During her career, she accumulated several European and world medals, asserting her dominance in butterfly events.

A POLISH STAR IN THE BUTTERFLY'S SKY

Otylia is famous for being one of the most accomplished butterfly swimmers of her generation. She not only shone at the Olympic level, but she also set world records, making her an iconic figure in Polish swimming. Her unique combination of power, technique and determination made her stand out from the rest, and she became an inspiration to many young swimmers in Poland and beyond.

In addition to her exploits in the pool, Otylia has shown great generosity outside of it. After winning a gold medal at the 2004 Olympics, she put her medal up for auction, donating the entire funds to a children's hospital in Poland, demonstrating her commitment to charitable causes. This action was praised not only in Poland, but also internationally, showing that she was not only a champion in the water, but also a true hero outside of it.

In October 2005, she was the victim of a serious car accident in which her brother died. She was seriously injured there, both physically and morally.

#50

JANET EVANS
"MISS PERPETUAL MOTION"

BORN ON AUGUST 28, 1971 IN FULLERTON, CALIFORNIA, UNITED STATES.

Janet Evans is an undisputed swimming legend, holding four Olympic gold medals and numerous world records. She won the 400m, 800m freestyle and 400m individual medley at the 1988 Seoul Olympics. Four years later, in Barcelona, she successfully defended her 800m freestyle title.

THE INDOMITABLE JANET EVANS

Her nickname, "Miss Perpetual Motion", reflects her inexhaustible endurance in the water. Evans dominated women's distance swimming in the late 1980s and early 1990s, setting world records that stood for decades. Her career illustrates the importance of technique and perseverance, as despite her small stature, she managed to outperform her competitors.

Evans is credited with breaking stereotypes about the "ideal" body shape of swimmers. Her distinctive technique and fast pace brought her many successes, but it was her incredible endurance that truly set her apart. One of her most memorable moments was when she beat the East German, considered unbeatable, in Seoul in 1988. In 1996 in Atlanta, despite not winning a medal, she had the honor of passing the Olympic torch to Muhammad Ali during the opening ceremony, a poignant moment that marked Olympic history.

Janet never enjoyed butterfly swimming, despite her excellence in freestyle and individual medley.

Throughout these pages, we have swum side by side with the titans of swimming, felt the pressure of the water and the beating of their hearts.

Each story reminds us of the power of determination, the importance of dreams and the beauty of effort.

As you close this book, remember that every length, every splash and every breath tells a story, the story of a relentless quest for excellence.

May these stories continue to inspire the swimmers of tomorrow and touch the hearts of all those who love sport.

Share your reactions with us after discovering or rediscovering these 50 legends.
Visit us on our networks:

Printed in Great Britain
by Amazon